John S. C. Abbott

The History of the Civil War in America

John S. C. Abbott

The History of the Civil War in America

ISBN/EAN: 9783337427641

Printed in Europe, USA, Canada, Australia, Japan

Cover: Foto ©ninafisch / pixelio.de

More available books at **www.hansebooks.com**

OF THE

CIVIL WAR IN AMERICA;

COMPRISING A FULL AND IMPARTIAL ACCOUNT OF THE

ORIGIN AND PROGRESS OF THE REBELLION,

OF THE VARIOUS

NAVAL AND MILITARY ENGAGEMENTS,

OF THE

Heroic Deeds Performed by Armies and Individuals,

AND OF

TOUCHING SCENES IN THE FIELD, THE CAMP, THE HOSPITAL, AND THE CABIN.

BY JOHN S. C. ABBOTT,

AUTHOR OF "LIFE OF NAPOLEON," "HISTORY OF THE FRENCH REVOLUTION," "MONARCHIES OF CONTINENTAL EUROPE," &c

ILLUSTRATED WITH MAPS, DIAGRAMS, AND NUMEROUS STEEL ENGRAVINGS OF

BATTLE SCENES,

FROM ORIGINAL DESIGNS BY DARLEY, AND OTHER EMINENT ARTISTS,

AND PORTRAITS OF DISTINGUISHED MEN.

SOLD ONLY BY DISTRIBUTING AGENTS.

NEW YORK:
PUBLISHED BY HENRY BILL.
1862.

LIST OF ILLUSTRATIONS.

PORTRAITS.

Hon. Abraham Lincoln.
Lieut. Gen. Winfield Scott.
Major Gen. George B. McClellan.
 " " John C. Fremont.
 " " H. W. Halleck.
 " " Franz Sigel.
 " " Benj. F. Butler.
 " " A. E. Burnside.
Commodore A. H. Foote.
Hon. Stephen A. Douglas,
  and others.

BATTLE SCENES.

Bombardment of Fort Sumter.
Battle of "Bull Run."
 " " Wilson's Creek.
Bombardment of Port Royal.
Storming of Fort Donelson.
Battle of Newberne.
 " " Pittsburgh Landing.
Engagement between the Monitor and Merrimac.
Capture of New Orleans,
  and others.

CHAPTER III.

THE WAR COMMENCED.

ENERGY OF THE CONSPIRATORS.—VIEWS OF SECESSIONISTS AND UNIONISTS.—TESTIMONY OF WEBSTER AND CLAY.—IGNOMINIOUS CONDUCT OF THE TRAITORS.—INAUGURATION OF PRESIDENT LINCOLN.—ANECDOTE.—FALL OF SUMTER.—UPRISING OF THE NORTH.—DEVELOPMENTS OF TREASON.—RESPONSE TO THE CALL FOR 75,000 VOLUNTEERS.—NOBLE SPEECH OF SENATOR DOUGLAS.—UNION OF ALL PARTIES.—TREACHERY OF REBELS IN VIRGINIA.—DESTRUCTION OF GOSPORT NAVY YARD.

ON the 22d of February, four days after the inauguration of Jefferson Davis, in Montgomery, the Collector of Customs, appointed by the rebel government in Charleston, S. C., issued the manifesto, that all vessels, from any State out of the Confederacy, would be treated as foreign vessels, and subject to the port dues and other charges established by the laws of the Confederate States. Thus, by a stroke of the pen, the immense commerce of the Northern States was declared to be foreign commerce, beneath the guns of the forts which the United States had reared, at an expense of millions of dollars.

As these outrages were progressing, the people of the Free States were waiting quietly, but with intense latent emotion, for the inauguration of President Lincoln. Nothing could be hoped for while Mr. Buchanan remained in the presidential chair; and *he* was probably more impatient than any other man in the United States, for the hour to arrive which would release him from the burdens of an office, which were infinitely too heavy for him to bear. He was apparently the unwilling servant of the Secessionists, and could not escape from the toils, in which he had become involved. But the Secessionists had no idea of allowing President Lincoln to be inaugurated. Though frustrated in their plan of securing his assassination, on his passage to the Capital, they were quite confident of their ability to seize Washington, and make it the metropolis of their Confederacy. One of the leading New York journals, under date of January 1, said:

"It is now well known, that military companies have been organized and drilled, for months past, in Maryland and Virginia, some of them under the eye of an officer of the regular army, and that the distinct object of their organization is, to aid in the seizure of Washington City, or the prevention, by force, of Lincoln's inauguration. Some of the less prudent of their leaders boast, in private circles, that they have five thousand well armed and organized men, ready to strike the blow instantly, upon the concerted signal being given."

Very energetic secret societies were organized, all through the Southern States, under the names of "Minute Men," "Vigilance Committees," and "Knights of the Golden Circle," pledged to sustain the Southern Confederacy, to extend the institution of slavery, and to watch over, and, if necessary, to exterminate all suspected of disaffection. Great numbers of men, who ventured to speak freely, were treated with every indignity, and hung. The Hon. Mr. Iverson, of Georgia, stated boastfully in the Senate of the United States, "A Senator from Texas has told me that a great many of those free debaters were hanging from the trees of that country." Future generations will find it hard to believe that in a civilized community such atrocities could be committed as were enacted by the advocates of slavery at the South.

Very great ability was displayed by the leaders of this conspiracy. They were men of thought, of wealth, and were long accustomed to the exercise of power. They were few in numbers, and could thus act with almost the energy of a single despotic mind. Robert Toombs, of Georgia, by his talent in debate, his self-confidence, and his imperious, inexorable will, held Cobb, Crawford, and Iverson, as the willing vassals of his baronial spirit, and thus molded as he pleased the State of Georgia. When Mr. Iverson, of Georgia, withdrew from the Senate, he uttered the following arrogant menace :

"Georgia is one of six States, which, in less than sixty days, have dissolved their connection with the Federal Union, and declared their separate independence. Steps are now in progress, to form a Confederacy of their own, and, in a few weeks at furthest, a provisional government will be formed, giving them ample powers for their own defence, with power to enter into negotiations with other nations, to make war, to conclude peace, to form treaties, and to do all other things which independent nations may of right do. Provision will be made for admission of other states to the new Union, and it is confidently believed that, within a few months, all the Southern States of the late Confederacy will be formed into a Union far more homogeneous, and, therefore, far more stable than the one now broken up.

"You may acquiesce in the revolution, and acknowledge the independence of a great Confederacy, or you may make war on the seceding States, and attempt to force them back. If you acknowledge our independence, and treat us as one of the nations of the earth, you can have friendly relations and intercourse with us ; you can have an equitable division of the public property and of the existing public debt of the United States. But if you make war upon us, we will seize and hold all the public property in our borders, and in our reach, and we will never pay one dollar of the public debt, for the law of nations will extinguish all public and private obligations between the States.

"The first Federal gun that is fired upon the seceding States—the first drop of blood of any of their people, shed by the Federal troops—will cancel every public and private obligation of the South, which may be due either to the Federal government or to the northern people. We care not in what shape or form, or under what pretext you undertake *coercion*. We shall consider *all* efforts to exercise authority over us, as acts of war, and shall meet and resist them, accordingly. You may send armies to invade us by land, or you may send ships to blockade our ports, and destroy our trade and commerce with other nations. You may abolish our ports of entry, and by an act of Congress, attempt to collect the Federal revenues by ships of war. You may do all or any of these or similar acts. They will be acts of war, and so understood and considered, and, in whatever shape you make war, we will fight you."

The views of the Secessionists can not be better expressed than in the above extracts. The following speech, delivered by the Hon. Mr. Doolittle, of Wisconsin, in the House of Representatives, on the 27th of December, contains in briefest compass the views of the Unionists. It is so important, that the true nature of the conflict should be rightly understood, that we introduce this comprehensive statement, even at the risk of a slight repetition.

"The Constitution of the United States speaks in language clear enough that it is not in the power of one out of ten, or of one hundred, or of all the citizens of a State, to annul an act of Congress, because the Constitution of the United States and an act in pursuance of it is a supreme law of that State, and binding upon every citizen of that State, and every citizen must act at his peril. Now if this doctrine is true, that a State by its own mere motion can assemble in convention a mass of its citizens, by resolutions dissolve its connection with the Federal Government, and put an end to the supremacy of the Constitution and laws of the United States, several other consequences must follow. If one State can secede from all the rest, I suppose the Senator from Louisiana will not deny but that all the rest can secede from one, and that of necessity gives to this Government the power to expel a State. Your right of secession involves the right of expulsion.

"Let us go a little further, and see how this doctrine would apply in time of war. We were engaged in a war with Great Britain in 1812, and the New England States, it is said, were rather disaffected, and met in Convention at Hartford. Now, if the doctrine of the gentleman is correct, any of the New England States could have resolved itself out at its pleasure, and gone over to the enemy. Our fortresses in Boston harbor, which we had manned, built, and filled with munitions and guns, they might have withdrawn from and surrendered to the enemy, and turned our own guns upon us.

"This is the consequence of this doctrine. But, again, take it in time of peace. Apply the doctrine to Pennsylvania, that she, by a simple resolution of her people, can withdraw from the United States. She could cut off all the mail routes going across Pennsylvania, and we could not go from Virginia to New York without going across a foreign country. So, too, with Illinois; if this doctrine is correct, we of the North-West could be cut off entirely from the East; and especially if the Union is to be broken up, we could not go to New York except by leave of Illinois; or without going through the State of Kentucky; and you propose to make that a foreign jurisdiction.

"Apply this doctrine further. How is it with Florida, a little State of the Gulf that has 50,000 white inhabitants—almost as many as some of the counties in the State where I live! We purchased this peninsula, and paid for it, to get rid of the foreign jurisdiction over it—also to get possession of the Key, and command the entrance to the Gulf. We paid $35,000,000 to take the Seminoles off from it, and now these 50,000 people, whom the good people of the United States permitted to go there and settle their territories—they had hardly population enough to be admitted as a State, but we have admitted them to full fellowship—Florida now attempts, by mere resolution of her people gathered together, to resolve herself out of the Union, and take all those fortresses, which we have spent thousands of dollars to make, with all our own guns, and turn them against us?

"How is it with Louisiana? The Government of the United States upon wise national principles of great national policy, purchased from the Emperor of France, or the First Consul, the Territory of Louisiana, at an expense of $15,000,000. We purchased it to obtain possession of the great valley of the Mississippi, and above all things, to hold the mouth of that river which controls all its commerce, and discharges it upon the high seas of the world. Now, can it be contended here that because the people whom the Federal Government has permitted to go in there, and occupy its lands, and permitted to be introduced into the family of this reunion, that she, in a moment of passion and excitement, by the mere resolution of her citizens, can resolve herself outside of the confederacy, declare that she is a foreign power, and take with her the control of the mouths of the Mississippi. I tell you, Mr. President, and I tell the Senator from Louisiana, that if any such doctrine had been understood when Louisiana was admitted, she would never have been admitted. I tell you, sir, if any such doctrine had been asserted, her people would never have been permitted to take possession of the swamps of Louisiana. They will not willingly consent that she should hold the mouths of the Mississippi, and thus control the commerce that goes out into the Gulf.

"How has it been with Texas? The Federal Government admitted Texas at a time when she had a sparse population, and there were many debts against her treasury, and her credit was impaired and broken. We took her, as one of the States, into this Confederacy. The result of her annexation brought the Mexican war, which cost us 40,000 lives and nearly $100,000,000. Now, when we have made her a good State, built fortifications, paid her debts and raised her to a position of a State in this Confederacy, with prospects as glorious, perhaps more so than any other Southern State, is she now, in a single hour or moment of passion, to resolve herself out of the Union and become a foreign power? Suppose we had paid $200,000,000 for Cuba, and acquired her, with all her fortifications, she could now go out, and turn our own guns against us? What is all our great boasted nationality? Is it a farce and a delusion?

"Gentlemen sometimes complain that the Republican party are disposed to do injustice to the citizens of the South, and to their social institutions especially. But what has been the history of the Government since it was formed under the Constitution? We have acquired Florida, Louisiana, Texas, and the Territory from Mexico. We have surrendered a part of Maine, and given up our claim to a large part of Oregon. Florida cost us $40,000,000. It has been given up to the social institutions of the South. We purchased Louisiana Territory, and two-thirds of the good land has been given up to the social institutions of the South. The annexation of Texas, the war with Mexico, and the acquisition of all those territories from Mexico, may be regarded as one transaction. Now I ask you, gentlemen, in all fairness and candor, to say whether we have not surrendered to your social institutions, your full share, comparing the number of persons who are employed in your system of labor, with the free white citizens of the United States? When you speak of injustice, it is without foundation. You have had your full share, and more than your share, of the Territories we have acquired from the beginning up to this hour.

"I am sick and tired of hearing gentlemen stand up here and complain of the injustice done to this institution of the South. There is no foundation for it in our history—none whatever. * * * What do we deny to you that we do not deny to ourselves? What single right have I in New Mexico that you have not? You say this law excludes your social institution. So it excludes our banking institutions and our manufacturing corporations. Your social institution is a kind of close corporation, existing under the laws of your States, not existing by the common law of the country. We deny you no right which we do not deny ourselves. * * * If we acquire Territory, you are asking too much when you ask us to convert it to Slave Territory. It is impossible that we can have peace upon any such doctrine as that. You must allow the Free Territories to remain free. We will not interfere with your institution where it exists. Sir, that is peace. I repeat, that non-interference by the General Government or by the Free State men, with Slavery in the States, and non-interference by the General Government or by the slaveholders, against freedom in the Territories, is peace."

In the spirit of these remarks, the Hon. Daniel Webster had said, in one of his latest speeches, made at Buffalo, May 22, 1851:

"If the South wish any concession from me, they won't get it—not a hair's breadth of it. If they come to my house for it, they will not find it. I concede nothing * * * No matter what may be said at the Syracuse Convention, or any other assemblage of insane persons, I never would consent that there should be one foot of Slave Territory beyond what the old Thirteen States had at the time of the formation of the Union. Never, never! The man can't show his face to me, and prove that I ever departed from that doctrine. He would sneak away, or slink away, or hire a mercenary Heep, that he might say, what a mercenary apostate from liberty Daniel Webster has become. He knows himself to be a hypocrite and falsifier. * * * All that I now say is, that, *with the blessing of God, I will not now or hereafter, before the country or the world, consent to be numbered among those who introduced new slave-power into the Union. I will do all in my power to prevent it.*"

Henry Clay was equally explicit upon this point of admitting slavery into the free territory of the United States. "So long," said he, "as God allows the vital current to flow through my veins, I will never, *never*, NEVER, by word or thought, by mind or will, aid in admitting one rood of free territory to the everlasting curse of human bondage." And he was no less emphatic in denouncing the insane doctrine of secession. "If any one state," said he, "or a portion of the people of any state, choose to place themselves in military array against the government of the Union, I am for trying the strength of the government. I am for ascertaining whether we have a government or not; practical, efficient; capable of maintaining its authority, and of upholding the interests which belong to a government. Nor am I to be alarmed or dissuaded from any such course by intimations of the spilling of blood."

Upon the retirement of the traitor Floyd from the government to join the rebels, Joseph Holt, one of the noblest sons of Kentucky, was entrusted with the portfolio of the War Department. In coöperation with General Scott, immediate measures were adopted to protect Washington from the menaced capture by the Rebels. This unexpected vigor greatly alarmed the Secessionists. More loudly than ever, the cry of "No coercion" rang through the land. On the 18th of February, Mr. Holt addressed a letter to the President, in reply to a resolution of the House, inquiring into the state of the defences in Washington. The following extracts from this letter give a vivid description of the condition of affairs at that time:

"The scope of the question submitted by the House will be sufficiently met by dealing with the facts as they exist, irrespective of the cause from which they have proceeded. That revolution has been distinguished by a boldness and completeness of success, rarely equaled in the history of civil commotions. Its overthow of the Federal authority has not only been sudden and widespread, but has been marked by excesses which have alarmed all, and been sources of profound humiliation to a large portion of the American people. Its history is a history of surprises, and treacheries, and ruthless spoliations. The forts of the United States have been captured and garrisoned, and hostile flags unfurled upon their ramparts. Its arsenals have been seized, and the vast amount of public arms they contained appropriated to the use of the captors, while more than half a million of dollars, found in the mint at New Orleans, have been unscrupulously applied to replenish the coffers of Louisiana. Officers in command of revenue cutters of the United States, have been prevailed on to violate their trusts, and surrender the property in their charge; and instead of being branded for their crimes, they, and the vessels they betrayed, have been cordially received into the service of the seceded States.

"At what time the armed occupation of Washington City became a part of the revolutionary programme is not certainly known; more than six weeks ago, the impression had already extensively obtained, that a conspiracy for the accomplishment of this guilty purpose was in process of formation, if not fully matured. The earnest endeavors made by men known to be devoted to the revolution, to hurry Virginia and Maryland out of the Union, were regarded as preparatory steps for the subjugation of Washington. This plan was in entire harmony with the aim and spirit of those seeking the subversion of the Government, since no more fatal blow at its existence could be struck than the permanent and hostile possession of the seat of its power. It was in harmony, too, with the avowed designs of the revolutionists, which looked to the formation of a confederacy of all the Slave States, and necessarily to the conquest of the capital within their limits.

"In view of the violence and turbulent disorders already exhibited in the South, the public mind could not reject such a scheme as at all improbable. That a belief in its existence was entertained by multitudes there can be no doubt, and this belief I fully shared. My conviction rested not only on the facts already alluded to, but upon information, some of which was of a most conclusive character, that reached the Government from many parts of the country, not merely expressing the prevalence of the opinion that such an organization had been formed, but also often furnishing the plausible grounds on which the opinion was based. Superadded to these proofs were the oft-repeated declarations of men in high political positions here, and who were known to have intimate affiliations with the revolution, if, indeed, they did not hold its reins in their hands, to the effect that Mr. Lincoln would not, or should not, be inaugurated at Washington. Such declarations from such men could not be treated as empty bluster. They were the solemn utterances of those who well understood the import of their words, and who, in the exultation of their temporary victories gained over their country's flag in the South, felt assured that events would soon give them the power to verify their predictions. Simultaneously with these prophetic warnings, a Southern journal of large circulation and influence, and which is published near the City of Washington, advocated its seizure as a possible political necessity.

"The nature and power of the testimony thus accumulated may be best estimated by the effect produced upon the popular mind. Apprehensions for the safety of the capital were communicated from points near and remote, by men unquestionably reliable and loyal. The resident population became disquieted, and the repose of many families in the city was known to be disturbed by painful anxieties. Members of Congress, too, men of calm and comprehensive views, and of undoubted fidelity to their country, frankly expressed their solicitude to the President and to this department, and formally insisted that the defenses of the capital should be strengthened. With such warnings, it could not be forgotten that, had the early admonitions which reached here in regard to the designs of lawless men upon the forts of Charleston harbor, been acted on by sending forward adequate reënforcements before the revolution began, the disastrous political complications that ensued might not have occurred.

"Impressed by these circumstances and considerations, I earnestly besought you to allow the concentration at this city of a sufficient military force, to preserve the public peace from all the dangers that seemed to threaten it. An open manifestation on the part of the Administration of a determination, as well as of the ability to maintain the laws, would, I was convinced, prove the surest, as also the most pacific means of baffling and dissolving any conspiracy that might have been organized. It was believed, too, that the highest and most solemn responsibility resting upon a President withdrawing from the Government, was to secure to his successor a peaceful inauguration. So deeply, in my judgment, did this duty concern the whole country and the fair fame of our institutions, that to guarantee its faithful discharge, I was persuaded no preparation could be too determined or too complete. The presence of the troops alluded to in the resolution, is the result of the conclusion arrived at by yourself and Cabinet, on the propositions submitted to you by this department.

"Already this display of life and loyalty on the part of your Administration, has produced the happiest effects. Public confidence has been restored, and the feverish apprehension which it was so mortifying to contemplate has been banished. Whatever may have been the machinations of deluded, lawless men, the execution of their purposes has been suspended, if not altogether abandoned, in view of preparations which announce more impressively than words, that this Administration is alike able and resolved, to transfer in peace to the President-elect the authority that, under the Constitution, belongs to him. To those, if such there be, who desire the destruction of the Republic, the presence of these troops is necessarily offensive; but those who sincerely love our institutions cannot fail to rejoice that, by this timely precaution, they have possibly escaped the deep dishonor which they must have suffered had the Capital, like the forts and arsenals of the South, fallen into the hands of revolutionists, who have found this great Government weak only because, in the exhaustless beneficence of its spirit, it has refused to strike even in its own defence, lest it should wound the aggressors.

"I have the honor to be, very respectfully, your obedient servant,

"JOSEPH HOLT, *Secretary of War.*"

Northern men had so generally been engaged in lucrative employments of industry, that comparatively few sought offices in the army or the navy, where, in a period of profound peace, there was but little scope for enterprise, and where neither wealth nor fame was to be won. But the sons of Southern planters, with nothing opening before them but an indolent life, were eager for these offices. The consequence was that now, in our hour of trial, the large proportion of the officers, in both the army and navy, were from the slaveholding States, and were eager to coöperate with their friends in revolutionizing the government. One after another they resigned their commissions, and entered the service of the Confederacy, where they were nominally reinstated in the possession of the same rank and pay which they had been enjoying. The resignation of men unblushingly avowing their treasonable intent, was accepted by Secretary Toucey, and they were honorably discharged.

One Breshwood, a Virginian, was in command of the United States revenue cutter *McLelland.* He infamously surrendered his vessel to the rebels at New Orleans. Capt. J. J. Morrison followed the same ignoble example, by surrendering the revenue cutter *Cass* to the rebels at Mobile. Gen. John A. Dix, one of America's untitled noblemen, just then appointed

Secretary of the Treasury, sent a secret agent, Hemphil Jones, to endeavor to rescue these vessels from their perfidious commanders. To this agent he gave the spirited order, " to shoot down on the spot any man who attempted to haul down the American Flag."

When great depravity is developed, great nobility of character also becomes conspicuous. Lieut. John N. Maffit was in command of the Crusader at Mobile. His steam gunboat was exposed to the fire of Fort Morgan, which the Rebels had just seized. He was commanded to surrender his vessel to the "Alabama Navy."

" I may be overpowered," was his reply, " but in that event what will be left of the Crusader will not be worth taking."

He rescued the vessel, which subsequently rendered signal service in the Gulf. Capt. Porter was ordered by Lieut. J. H. Hamilton, of South Carolina, to surrender his ship to the Rebels. His reply, dated United States Ship St. Marys, Panama Bay, Feb. 3, 1861, contains the following noble sentiments :

" You, sir, have called upon your brother officers, not only to become traitors to their country, but to betray their sacred trust, and deliver up the ships under their command. This infamous appeal would, in ordinary times, be treated with the contempt it deserves. But I feel it a duty I owe myself and brother officers, with whom I am associated, to reply and state, that all under my command are true and loyal to the 'Stars and Stripes,' and to the Constitution. My duty is plain before me. The constitutional government of the United States, has entrusted me with the command of this beautiful ship, and before I will permit any other flag than the 'Stars and Stripes' to fly at her peak, I will fire a pistol in her magazine, and blow her up. This is my answer to your infamous letter."

The week preceding the 4th of March, when Mr. Lincoln was to be inaugurated, was one of intense solicitude and excitement. The air was filled with rumors of conspiracies, to prevent the inauguration by a bloody tumult, and by seizing the Capital. Washington was thronged with strangers, many from the South, armed with bowie-knives and revolvers. Apparently there would have been but little difficulty in a few thousand men, at a concerted signal, making a rush which would sweep all opposition before them. Gen. Scott and Secretary Holt were in the meantime making quiet, but effectual preparations, to meet any emergency. An imposing military escort was provided to conduct the President to the Capitol, and back again, after the inauguration, to the White House.

The eventful morning dawned propitiously. At an early hour, Pennsylvania Avenue was thronged, the centre of attraction being Willard's Hotel, where, thus far, the President elect had occupied apartments. The procession began to form about 9 o'clock. It was very brilliant and imposing. One very striking feature was a large triumphal car, the Constitution, bearing thirty-four very beautiful girls, robed in white, as representatives of the several States. It was thus manifest that the government had no idea of recognizing the Union as dissolved. Mr. Buchanan and Mr. Lincoln sat, side by side, in the carriage. They ascended the steps of the Capitol arm in arm. It was noticed that Mr. Buchanan looked pale, sad, and nervous; he sighed audibly and frequently. Mr. Lincoln's face was slightly flushed, and his lips compressed, with an expression of much gravity and firmness.

The President elect took his stand upon the platform of the portico of the Capitol. The Supreme Court, the Senate, the House of Representatives, the Foreign Ministers, and a vast crowd of privileged persons, soon occupied every seat. A countless throng filled the grounds below, a surging mass of friends and foes. There were exasperated secessionists, watching for a chance to strike a blow, and pure patriots ready to repel that blow, at any hazard of life. Senator Baker of Oregon, introduced the President to the people. Mr. Lincoln then, with strength of voice which arrested every ear, delivered his inaugural address. Speaking of secession, he said:

"Physically speaking we can not separate,—we can not remove our respective sections from each other, nor build an impassable wall between them. A husband and wife may be divorced, and go out of the presence and beyond the reach of each other; but the different parts of our country can not do this. They can not but remain face to face; and intercourse, either amicable or hostile, must continue between them. Is it possible, then, to make that intercourse more advantageous or more satisfactory after separation than before? Can aliens make treaties easier than friends can make laws? Can treaties be more faithfully enforced between aliens, than laws can among friends? Suppose you go to war; you can not fight always, and when, after much loss on both sides, and no gain on either, you cease fighting, the identical questions, as to terms of intercourse, are again upon you."

In reference to the policy to be pursued he said, "To the extent of my ability I shall take care, as the Constitution itself expressly enjoins upon me, that the laws of the Union be faithfully executed in all the States. Doing this I deem to be only a simple duty on my part. I shall perfectly perform it, so far as is practicable, unless my rightful masters, the American people, shall withhold the requisition, or, in some authoritative manner, direct the contrary. I trust this will not be regarded as a menace, but only as the declared purpose of the Union, that it will constitutionally defend and maintain itself. In doing this there need be no bloodshed or violence, and there shall be none, unless it is forced upon the national authority. The power confided to me will be used to hold, occupy, and possess the property and places belonging to the government, and collect the duties and imposts; but beyond what may be necessary for these objects, there will be no invasion,—no using of force against or among the people anywhere.

Mr. Lincoln closed his noble inaugural with the following words, alike firm and conciliatory: "In your hands, my dissatisfied fellow-countrymen, and not in mine, is the momentous issue of civil war. The government will not assail you. You can have no conflict without being yourselves the aggressors. You have no oath registered in heaven to destroy the government; while I shall have the most solemn one to 'preserve, protect, and defend it.' I am loth to close. We are not enemies, but friends. We must not be enemies. Though passion may have strained, it must not break our bonds of affection. The mystic chords of memory, stretching from every battle-field and patriot grave, to every living heart and hearth-stone, all over this broad land, will yet swell the chorus of the Union, when again touched, as surely they will be, by the better angels of our nature."

The oath of office was then administered by Chief Justice Taney; the procession was again formed, and Mr. Lincoln was escorted to the White House. Though President Lincoln used with the utmost sincerity the language of conciliation, he was too well informed to believe that the South could be conciliated. The following anecdote, which he once narrated with great effect, proves that he well understood the deadly nature of the conflict.

" I once knew," he said, " a good sound churchman, whom we will call Brown, who was in a committee to erect a bridge over a very dangerous and rapid river. Architect after architect failed, and, at last, Brown said, he had a friend named Jones, who had built several bridges, and could build this. 'Let us have him in,' said the committee. In came Jones. 'Can you build this bridge, sir?' 'Yes,' replied Jones. 'I could build a bridge to the infernal regions if necessary.' The sober committee were horrified. But when Jones retired, Brown thought it but fair to defend his friend. 'I know Jones so well,' said he, 'and he is so honest a man, and so good an architect, that if he states, soberly and positively, that he can build a bridge to Hades, why, I believe it. But I have my doubts about the abutment on the infernal side.'" So Mr. Lincoln added, "When politicians said they could harmonize the northern and southern wings of the democracy, why, I believed them. But I had my doubt about the abutment on the southern side."

The Charleston Courier, under date of February 12th, says, "The South *might* after uniting under the new Confederacy, treat the disorganized and demoralized Northern States as *insurgents*, and deny them recognition. But if peaceful division ensues, the South, after taking the Federal Capital, and being recognized by all foreign powers, as the government *de facto*, can, if they see proper, recognize the Northern Confederacy, or Confederacies, and enter into treaty stipulations with them. Were this not done it would be difficult for the Northern States to take a place among nations, and their flag would not be respected or recognized."

The Mobile Advertiser, of about the same date, said, "The Spartans were small in number, but each man a host. Their narrow territory was peopled by two classes proper,—laborers and fighters. The laborers were slaves, and the freemen fighters. The South could detach one-half of its whole male population to wage war, with as much ease as the North could one-fifth; and in case of need the proportionate array of fighters which we could marshal would astonish the world."

The result has proved this statement correct. The slaves furnished the supplies for the war. Though in heart with the North, they were compelled to work for the support of their masters who went to the field. Every voice from the South indicated the undoubting confidence with which the conspirators were moving toward the accomplishment of their plans.

Effectual arrangements were now made for the bombardment and capture of Sumter. Iron-clad batteries had been reared so numerous and so formidable, that no wooden frigate could pass them, and thus it became impossible to send any assistance to the heroic little garrison there beleaguered. On the 12th of April, the rebels sent a demand to the starving garrison to surrender. Major Anderson replied that "his sense of honor and his obligations to the government would prevent his compliance;" but at the same time he admitted that the garrison were nearly starved out, and that, if no supplies reached them before the 15th, they would then be compelled to surrender.

At half past four o'clock on the morning of the 12th of April, the rebels opened the fire upon a fort and the flag of the United States, thus commencing, with tremendous energy, all the horrors of civil war. In that frenzied and exultant hour, little did they imagine the misery and ruin they were inviting upon their own heads. The government, in the hands of the traitors who dominated over the councils of President Buchanan, had succumbed so ignobly to menaces of the conspirators, that they now looked upon that government with contempt, and had no apprehension that it would ever manifest sufficient life to chastise them for their treason.

The fire was almost simultaneously opened upon the fort, from Fort Moultrie, the iron-clad floating battery in the harbor, and from heavy batteries on Mount Pleasant and on Cummings Point. A small fleet, with supplies, was seen outside the harbor, but it was certain destruction for the ships to attempt to pass the forts and batteries, and they could, consequently, render no assistance in the conflict. For two hours the little garrison, secure in their casemates, received the bombardment without reply, solid shot crashing down their walls, and shells exploding everywhere around them. After taking a comfortable breakfast, at half past six o'clock, the command was divided into three reliefs, and the first relief, under Captain Doubleday and Lieutenant Snyder, of the Engineer corps, opened the returning fire. The encircling batteries poured such a storm of shells upon the parapet that no one could stand there, and the guns in the casemates were mainly used. There is perhaps no work more exhausting than manning heavy guns. The garrison, enfeebled by months of siege, with but a scanty supply of provisions, having eaten that morning their very last biscuit, were in a poor condition to contend against an army of ten thousand men, stationed behind the strongest ramparts which modern science could construct. Less than one hundred men were thus arrayed against ten thousand.

Major Anderson, though aware that the fort must fall, yet resolved upon a heroic resistance, while taking the utmost care of his men. A sentinel was kept constantly upon the look-out, who cried out "shot" or "shell," at every shot the enemy made, and thus the men easily obtained shelter. It is difficult for one, not familiar with war, to imagine the power of the missiles which modern science has constructed. Solid walls of brick were crumbled down like powder. Cannons weighing thousands of pounds were thrown from their carriages by the explosion of shells. Red hot shot and bursting shells soon set the wooden barracks of the soldiers on fire, and nearly the whole interior of the fort blazed like a furnace. For thirty-six hours, this terrific bombardment continued all day and all night, with but occasional lulls, from the early dawn of Friday morning till near the close of Saturday afternoon. The garrison in Sumter soon became so exhausted, that they could make but a feeble response. An eye-witness thus describes the scene within the fort:

"The fire surrounded us on all sides. Fearful that the walls might crack, and the shells pierce and prostrate them, we commenced taking the powder out of the magazine before the fire had fully enveloped it. We took 96 barrels of powder out, and threw them into the sea, leaving 200 barrels in it. Owing to a lack of cartridges, we kept five men inside the magazine, sewing, as we wanted them, thus using up our shirts, sheets, blankets, and all the available material in the fort. When we were finally obliged to close the magazine, and our material for cartridges was exhausted, we were left destitute of any means to continue the contest. We had eaten our last biscuit thirty-six hours before. We came very near being stifled with the dense, livid smoke from the burning buildings. Many of the men lay prostrate on the ground, with wet handkerchiefs over their mouths and eyes, gasping for breath. It was a moment of imminent peril. If an eddy of wind had not ensued, we all, probably, should have been suffocated. The crashing of the shot, the bursting of the shells, the falling of walls, and the roar of the flames made a pandemonium of the fort. We nevertheless kept up a steady fire."

Such was the state of affairs, when, near the close of the day, a small boat suddenly made its appearance at one of the embrasures, with a white flag, and Major Wigfall, formerly a United States Senator from Texas, and who had been one of the most fierce and conspicuous of the Secessionists, was permitted to crawl through the embrasure. The fort was on fire, the garrison utterly exhausted, and yet the tattered banner of Stars and Stripes floated proudly and defiantly over the ruins. After some conference, and the arrival of another deputation, it was agreed that the garrison should surrender the fort, taking with them, as they retired at their leisure and in their own way, all their individual and company property, their side arms, and the war-scathed flag, which they were to salute with a hundred guns, before they hauled it down.

The battle now ceased. The fire was ere long extinguished, having destroyed nearly everything combustible, and the wearied men had a night of such rest as could be found in the midst of the ruins which surrounded them. About half past 9 o'clock on Sunday morning, the evacuation commenced. The booming of cannon echoed over the bay, as the heroic and indomitable band saluted the Flag sinking from its staff, and then, as with the proud step of victors, the band playing "Yankee Doodle" and "Hail Columbia," they marched out of the main gate, with the Stars and the Stripes waving over them, and entered the transport Isabel, which conveyed them to the United States Ship Baltic, in the offing, by which they were carried in triumph to New York.

Fort Sumter was the Bunker Hill of this Civil War. In both cases, a proud aristocracy were determined to subject this country to its sway. In both cases, the defeat was a glorious victory. This little band of heroes withstood the attack of an army, provided with the heaviest batteries which Europe and America could afford. For thirty-six hours they continued the unequal conflict. And then, when they had not another cartridge to fire, and not another biscuit to divide, they evacuated the ruins, the Stars and Stripes still waving over them, and they stepping proudly to the air of "Hail Columbia." The nation regarded it as a victory, and welcomed them as heroes. And the people of the United States will never cease to regard each member of the intrepid garrison of Fort Sumter with admiration and homage.

From the statistical report, given in the Charleston Mercury of May 3, it appears that the Rebels threw into and upon the fort, from fourteen batteries, 2361 solid shot, and 980 shells. Among the incidents of the battle related by an eye-witness, one is that a ten-inch shell entered the fort just above the magazine, cut its way through a block of granite, a foot thick, as if it had been cheese, and then exploded, casting a fragment of the shell, weighing twenty pounds, against the massive iron door of the magazine with such force, that the door was so bent that it could not be closed. Soon after this a red-hot shot passed quite through the outer wall of the magazine, and penetrated the inner wall to the depth of four inches, when it fell to the floor. All this time grains of powder, spilled by the men, were lying loosely about, so that it is a wonder, almost approaching to a miracle, that the magazine was not fired, and the fort and all its defenders blown into the air.

It is a marvelous fact, but one now apparently well authenticated, that during this long and terrific bombardment no one was killed on either side. After the battle was over, by the accidental explosion of a gun in saluting the national flag, one of the Federal soldiers was killed and several wounded. But in the battle, no one was seriously hurt. The Rebels had been for months preparing for the conflict, and the balls from Sumter which struck their batteries, cased, at a sharp angle, with railroad iron, glanced off, in the express language of an eye-witness, like marbles thrown by the hand of a child against the back of a tortoise. The men in Sumter were so few in number, and in casemates behind walls sixty feet high, and from twelve to fifteen feet thick, that it is not so very incredible that they should have escaped unharmed. And yet when we reflect that fifty tons weight of iron was thrown upon them with force which crumbled down the most massive masonry, it does indeed seem surprising that "nobody was hurt."

Three times the fort was on fire, and twice the flames were extinguished, by the whole garrison ceasing to fire, and passing along water. To do this it was necessary for the men to go outside the walls, and hand the buckets in through the port-holes, all the time exposed to the incessant fire from the batteries. The third time the flames burst out, all their efforts to extinguish them were baffled, and they burned until almost everything combustible was consumed. The scene in Charleston, during this bombardment, must have been such as can not easily be imagined. From the steeples, the house-tops, and battery, the whole bay was spread out before the eye; and never before, perhaps, was there so perfect a panorama of battle. One of the rebels, who was in Charleston at the time, thus describes the scene:

"At the gray of the morning on Friday, the roar of cannon broke upon the ear. The expected sound was answered by thousands. The houses were in a few minutes emptied of their excited occupants, and the living stream poured through all the streets leading to the wharves and battery. On reaching our beautiful promenade, we found it lined with ranks of eager spectators, and all the wharves, commanding a view of the battle, were crowded thickly with human forms. On no gala occasion have we ever seen so large a number of ladies on our Battery as graced the breezy walk on this eventful morning. There they stood, with palpitating hearts and pallid faces, watching the white smoke as it rose in wreaths, upon the soft twilight air, and breathing out fervent prayers for their gallant kinsfolk at the guns."

The avowed object of the rebels, in their attack upon Sumter, was to cross the Rubicon in the actual inauguration of civil war, and thus to "fire the heart of the South." It was supposed that the South, being thus committed, would be compelled, by pride, to continue the conflict, for southern pride would scorn to entertain the thought of apology and submission. This outrage upon our country's flag, this inauguration of civil war, which was to cost more than a hundred thousand lives, to impoverish countless families, and to imperil our very national existence, was received throughout the rebellious cities, with all the demonstrations of pride and joy. Those who still loved their country did not dare to utter a remonstrating word, for an iron tyranny crushed them.

But the uprising in the North was such as the world never witnessed before. The slaveholders at the South had so long been threatening blood and ruin, that the North had quite ceased to regard their menaces. There was hardly a man to be found in all the North, who had any idea that the Southern rebels would venture to commence civil war. The bombardment of Sumter created universal amazement and indignation. As the news of the insult to the national flag, of the battle, and of the capture of the fort by the rebels, was flashed along the wires, excitement, perhaps unparalleled in the history of the world, pervaded every city and hamlet, and almost every heart. All party distinctions seemed to be forgotten. There were henceforth but two parties in the land,—the rebels with their sympathizers, and the friends of the Union.

On the next day, Monday, April 15, the President issued a call for three months' service of 75,000 volunteers, and summoned an extra session of Congress to meet on the 4th of July. The response of the loyal States to this call for troops was prompt and cordial in the highest possible degree. Never perhaps were a people found less prepared for war, than were the people of the Northern States. Accustomed only to peace, and not anticipating any foe, many of the States had not even the form of a military organization. All the energies of the people were consecrated to the arts of industry, not to those of destruction. We had neither soldiers nor officers. The men who had received military education at West Point, weary of having absolutely nothing to do, but to wear away the irksome hours, in some fort on the shore or in the wilderness, had generally engaged in other pursuits. They had become civil engineers, railroad superintendents, instructors in scientific schools, and thus had become in reality merely civilians who had studied the science and theory of war, but with no practical acquaintance with the duties of the field.

This was not our shame, but our glory. We were men of peace and industry, and of great prosperity. We had not dreamed that traitors would rise to plunge this happy land into anarchy, and to destroy this best government,—best notwithstanding all its imperfections,—earth has ever known. Floyd had emptied the arsenals, and placed the guns in the hands of the rebels. Our little standing army, consisting of but 10,755 men, officers and privates all told, he had scattered at almost illimitable distances over our vast frontier. Mr. Buchanan's Secretary of the Navy had equally dispersed the fleet ; in fact our neglected navy had fallen almost into decay. And more than all this, the majority of the officers in the army and in the navy, were men of slave-holding connections, many of whom openly avowed their sympathy with rebellion, and they had become so lost to all sense of honor, that the betrayal to the enemy of the Flag which they had sworn to protect,—a deed which all the rest of the world called *infamous*, they deemed *chivalrous*. Such was the condition of the North, when the war commenced.

Mr. Lincoln, in organizing his cabinet, had gratified the whole country by showing but little reference to party. Aware of the peril impending he had selected the ablest men wherever found, whose patriotism and zeal could not be doubted, to fill these important posts. William H. Seward of New York, was Secretary of State. Salmon P. Chase of Ohio, Secretary of the Treasury. Simon Cameron of Pennsylvania, Secretary of War. Gideon Welles of Connecticut, Secretary of the Navy. Montgomery Blair of Maryland, Postmaster General. Edward Bates of Missouri, Attorney General. Caleb B. Smith of Indiana, Secretary of the Interior. These were all patriots in whose ability and integrity the community in general, reposed confidence. Mr. Cameron thus describes the condition of the War Department, as he entered upon its duties :

" Upon my appointment to the position, I found the department destitute of all the means of defense ; without guns, and with little prospect of purchasing the *matériel* of war. I found the nation without an army, and I found scarcely a man throughout the whole War Department in whom I could put my trust. The Adjutant General deserted. The Quartermaster General ran off. The Commissary General was on his death-bed. More than half the clerks were disloyal. I remember that upon one occasion General Scott came to me, apparently in great mental tribulation. Said he, ' I have spent the most miserable day in my life ; a friend of my boyhood has just told me I am disgracing myself by staying here, and serving this fragment of the government, in place of going to Virginia, and serving under the banner of my native State ; and I am pained to death.' But the old hero was patriotic, loyal, and wise enough to say that his friend was wrong, and he was right in remaining where he was."

The conspirators, however, had been busy for years preparing for the conflict. In the rebel convention which met in South Carolina to consummate the conspiracy, Mr. Inglis, said, "Most of us have had this subject under consideration for the last twenty years." Mr. Keitt said, "I have been engaged in this movement ever since I entered political life." Mr. Rhett said, "It is nothing produced by Mr. Lincoln's election, or the non-execution of the fugitive slave law. It is a matter which has been gathering head for thirty years." In many of the States there was an efficient military organization, and the troops were under active drill. Agents had been despatched to England, to try to win sympathy there, and to enlist the coöperation of leading journals, by promises of free trade. Nothing which wealth or intrigue could accomplish, had been neglected by the traitors, to prepare the way for their great purpose. The Richmond Enquirer, to encourage the friends of the conspiracy with the assurance that all things were ripe for the outbreak, published the following notice, the more memorable, as proclaimed by a sheet which was the recognized mouth-piece of Floyd:

"The facts we are about to state are official and indisputable. Under a single order of the late Secretary of War, the Hon. Mr. Floyd, made during the last year, there were 115,000 improved muskets and rifles transferred from the Springfield armory, Mass., and Watervliet arsenal, N. Y., to different arsenals at the South. The total number of improved arms, thus supplied to five depositories in the South, by a single order of the late Secretary of War, was 114,868. In addition to this, the Memphis Appeal (Tenn.) stated, at the same time, that, by this action of Floyd, by the seizure of forts and arsenals, and by purchase from abroad, the rebel states had then, distributed at various convenient points, 707,000 stand of arms, and 200,000 revolvers.

The response from the loyal States to the President's call for troops was so enthusiastic, that far more men were ready to march than were called for, and millions of dollars were immediately offered to replenish the exhausted treasury. Within fifteen days, it is estimated that 350,000 volunteers offered themselves in defence of our national flag. In all the slaveholding States, even in those border States where the majority of the population were in favor of the Union, the conspirators had contrived to place their own friends in all the important offices. Missouri, Kentucky, and Tennessee were undoubtedly, by the popular vote, in large majority for the Union. But the Governors of these States assumed that the United States had no right to defend its own property and forts, or to protect its own troops, within the limits of the slaveholding States, now that they demanded the surrender of these forts and property, and the departure of these troops. C. M. Jackson, Governor of Missouri, in response to the President's call, said:

"Your requisition, in my judgment, is illegal, unconstitutional, and revolutionary in its objects, inhuman, and diabolical, and can not be complied with. Not one man will the State of Missouri furnish, to carry on such an unholy crusade."

B. Magoffin, Governor of Kentucky, responded in the following laconic note:

"Your dispatch is received. In answer, I say emphatically, that Kentucky will furnish no troops for the wicked purpose of subduing her sister Southern States."

Similar responses came from several of the Governors of States still professedly in the Union. But the people in these States rushed by tens of thousands to defend our common country, and overthrow the traitorous rulers who wished to carry them off into rebellion.

The news of the capture of Sumter was received by the Rebel Congress in Montgomery with the greatest exultation. An immense crowd serenaded Jeff. Davis and his Secretary of War, Leroy P. Walker, at the Exchange Hotel. Jeff. Davis was sick, probably sick at heart, in view of the woes which the rebellion was bringing upon the land. He had thought that the North would yield without a struggle. He saw now that a civil war had commenced of such magnitude, that it must deluge the land in blood, and that the chances were that the rebellion would be crushed. He was sick. There was no tonic in the tidings to raise his head from his pillow. But his Secretary, Mr. Walker, appeared upon the balcony, and, in an exultant speech, said:

"No man can tell where the war, commenced this day, will end. But I will prophecy that the flag which now flaunts the breeze here will float over the dome of the old Capitol at Washington, before the 1st of May. Let them try Southern chivalry, and test the extent of Southern resources, and it may float eventually over Faneuil Hall itself."

The unanimity with which the whole North arose, in this crisis, all party differences being merged in enthusiastic devotion to the Union, is one of the most extraordinary events of history. Men who but a few days before had been bitterly hostile, were at once seen standing side by side, upon the same platform, in earnest coöperation to resist the audacious rebellion. Senator Douglas, one of the candidates for the Presidency, at this crisis, came forward with zeal and power which will forever entitle him to the gratitude of his countrymen. The overwhelming majority of his party followed their illustrious leader in the magnanimity of his patriotism. On the 1st of May, Senator Douglas reached Chicago, Illinois, on his return from Washington. He was met at the depot, by an immense assemblage of citizens, who conducted him in a triumphal procession to the great "Wigwam," where ten thousand persons, of all parties, were seated awaiting him. The Senator addressed them in the following strain, which thrilled the heart of the nation, and which will give him ever-during and grateful remembrance.

"I beg you to believe that I will not do you or myself the injustice to think that this magnificent ovation is personal to myself. I rejoice to know that it expresses your devotion to the Constitution, the Union and the flag of our country. I will not conceal gratification at the uncontrovertible test this vast audience presents—that, what political differences or party questions may have divided us, yet you all had a conviction that, when the country should be in danger, my loyalty could be relied on. That the present danger is imminent, no man can conceal. If war must come—if the bayonet must be used to maintain the Constitution—I say before God, my conscience is clean. I have struggled long for a peaceful solution of the difficulty. I have not only tendered those States, what was theirs of right, but I have gone to the very extreme of magnanimity.

"The return we receive is war, armies marched upon our Capital, obstructions and dangers to our navigation, letters of marque, to invite pirates to prey upon our commerce, a concerted movement to blot out the United States of America from the map of the globe. The question is, Are we to maintain the country of our fathers, or allow it to be stricken down by those who, when they can no longer govern, threaten to destroy?

"What cause, what excuse do disunionists give us, for breaking up the best Government, on which the sun of heaven ever shed its rays? They are dissatisfied with the result of the Presidential election. Did they never get beaten before? Are we to resort to the sword when we get defeated at the ballot box? I understand it that the voice of the people expressed in the mode appointed by the Constitution, must command the obedience of every citizen. They assume, on the election of a particular candidate, that their rights are not safe in the Union. What evidence do they present of this? I defy any man to show any act on which it is based. What act has been omitted to be done? I appeal to these assembled thousands, that so far as the constitutional rights of slaveholders are concerned, nothing has been done, and nothing omitted, of which they can complain.

"There has never been a time from the day that Washington was inaugurated first President of these United States, when the rights of the Southern States stood firmer under the laws of the land than they do now; there never was a time when they had not as good cause for disunion as they have to-day. What good cause have they now that has not existed under every Administration?

"If they say the Territorial question—now, for the first time, there is no act of Congress prohibiting slavery anywhere. If it be the non-enforcement of the laws, the only complaints that I have heard, have been of the too vigorous and faithful fulfillment of the Fugitive Slave Law. Then what reason have they?

"The Slavery question is a mere excuse. The election of Lincoln is a mere pretext. The present secession movement is the result of an enormous conspiracy formed more than a year since, formed by leaders in the Southern Confederacy more than twelve months ago.

"But this is no time for the detail of causes. The conspiracy is now known. Armies have been raised, war is levied to accomplish it. There are only two sides to the question. Every man must be for the United States or against it. There can be no neutrals in this war; *only patriots or traitors.*

"Thank God, Illinois is not divided on this question. I know they expected to present a united South against a divided North. They hoped in the Northern States, party questions would bring civil war between Democrats and Republicans, when the South would step in, with her cohorts, aid one party to conquer the other, and then make easy prey of the victors. Their scheme was carnage and civil war in the North.

"There is but one way to defeat this. In Illinois it is being so defeated by closing up the ranks. War will thus be prevented on our own soil. While there was a hope of peace, I was ready for any reasonable sacrifice or compromise to maintain it. But when the question comes of war in the cotton fields of the South, or the corn fields of Illinois, I say the farther off the better.

"I have said more than I intended to say. It is a sad task to discuss questions so fearful as civil war; but sad as it is, bloody and disastrous as I expect it will be, I express it as my conviction before God, that it is the duty of every American citizen to rally around the flag of his country.

"I thank you again for this magnificent demonstration. By it you show you have laid aside party strife. Illinois has a proud position—united, firm, determined never to permit the Government to be destroyed."

Immediately after the fall of Sumter, on the 17th of April, and in response to the President's call for 75,000 men, Jefferson Davis, the head of a band of conspirators and rebels, who had not been recognized as a nation by any government on the globe, issued a proclamation authorizing privateers to be fitted out from all the ports of the South, to prey upon the vast commerce of the United States. The merchant marine of the United States, whitening the gulf, and spread over all seas, was utterly defenseless. And now the government began to feel the treachery which had dismantled and dispersed our fleet. We could send no convoys. We could blockade no ports. We had not a single half dozen vessels of war, which we could immediately call into service. Was ever a nation before so betrayed? And the very men in whom we had confided, whom the people had placed in the highest posts of office and of honor, had thus left us naked to our enemies. Within a few weeks the Rebels boasted that they had seized ships to the amount of several millions of dollars. Those which they could not conveniently carry into port, they plundered and burned at sea.

On the 19th of April, as a protection against this piratical proclamation, and as the nation's reply, the President announced the blockade of all the ports of the seceded States. And never before was a navy created with such magical rapidity. In less than three months over three hundred vessels of war, ploughing the waves beneath the Stars and Stripes, and the heroic men who trod their decks, were eager to avenge any insult to that flag, which never yet has been dishonored.

The Star of the West, an unarmed merchant steamer, which had attempted unavailingly to convey supplies to Fort Sumter, was afterwards sent to Indianola, Texas, with supplies of provisions for the United States troops in garrison there. These troops had been stationed along the frontier, to protect the Texans from invasion by the savages. On the night of April 17th, a band of eighty Rebels from Galveston, under the command of one Van Dorn, threw themselves, by stratagem, on board the ship, and seized it without a struggle. The crew were as little anticipating an attack, as they would have been in the harbor of New York. The ship was taken to Galveston, and being plundered of all its provisions, was put in commission as the Receiving Ship of the Confederate Navy, at New Orleans.

In the steamer, when captured, there were three free colored men from the North. They were taken to Montgomery, Alabama, the capital of the Confederacy, whose boasted corner-stone was slavery. Here, under the secession flag, they were sold at auction into endless slavery. Two of them, it was said, were husbands and fathers, having wives and children in New York. They are probably, while I write, if still living, toiling beneath the overseer's lash on some barbaric plantation in Alabama, with no hope of ever seeing wife or child again. These men were in the employ of the United States. They were sailing under the protection of its flag. Such were the outrages with which the rebels inaugurated civil war, exclaiming all the time, "No coercion; we only want to be let alone."

The rebels now prepared to make an immediate strike for the possession of Washington, before the North could find time to gather its forces for defense.

The Richmond Examiner, of April 23, says, "The capture of Washington City is perfectly within the power of Virginia and Maryland, if Virginia will only make the effort by her constituted authorities; nor is there a single moment to lose. The entire population pant for the onset. There never was half the unanimity among the people before, nor a tithe of the zeal upon any subject, that is now manifested to take Washington, and drive from it every Black Republican who is a dweller there. From the mountain tops and valleys to the shores of the sea, there is one wild shout of fierce resolve to capture Washington City, at all and every hazard. Our people can take it; they will take it; and Scott, the archtraitor, and Lincoln, the beast, combined, cannot prevent it."

In reference to the plot for the capture of Washington, the following facts are well authenticated. A conspiracy was formed by leading Virginians, with prominent Secessionists in Washington, and many traitors of influence and wealth in Baltimore, to accomplish the infamous and cowardly act in the following manner. Virginia did not then pretend to be out of the Union, and was fully represented in the House and also in the Senate.

The Virginians, at the head of between two and three thousand desperate men, were to make a rush upon Harper's Ferry, seize the arsenal there, which contained twenty-five thousand stand of arms, and thus supply themselves with an abundance of weapons and ammunition. They were then rapidly to descend the Potomac to Washington, and make a fierce onset in the streets of the city. Traitors there, in strong bands and armed to the teeth, were prepared to receive them. Incendiaries were appointed to fire the city at several points. In the midst of the uproar and terror of this sudden assault, the conspirators were to seize the most important government buildings, and convert them into fortresses, where they could bid defiance to any immediate attack from the bewildered government, and whence they could command the city.

In the meantime the conspirators in Baltimore were to cut off all communication with the North, by burning bridges, tearing up railways, and by seizing the post-office and telegraph stations. Should any troops attempt to descend from the North, for the rescue of the National metropolis, the mob was to be aroused to destroy them in the streets of Baltimore. At the same time troops were to be ready, from the South, to rush to the captured city, with infantry, artillery and cavalry, and to occupy all the important military stations. The star-spangled banner was to be torn from its proud position, and the secession banner was to be spread over the dome of the Capitol. Virginia and Maryland were thus to be dragged into secession, and Washington was to be the capital of the Southern Confederacy.

The Government were made acquainted with this plot, just on the eve of its execution. It did not seem possible to avert the menaced doom. Washington was filled with rebels. No reliance could be placed upon the militia. Perjured Southern traitors were occupying the most important posts in the army, and the Government knew not whom to trust. Never, perhaps, before, was a Government surrounded with more serious difficulties. A gentleman of high position, and intimately connected with the movements of the Government, and who was in Washington at this time, has given me the following account of some of the scenes which occurred there, in this hour of peril :

" On the 18th of April, 1861, it was confidentially made known among the loyal guests at Willard's Hotel, that a party of some twenty-five hundred men had arrived at or near Harper's Ferry, and that early on the evening of that day, the United States arms, in the arsenal at the Ferry, were to be seized, and the locomotives and cars of the Baltimore and Ohio Railroad Company were also to be taken, and an immediate descent to be made upon Washington.

" It was further stated that, on the near approach of said force, signals were to be made to the rebel occupants of the city of Washington, who were in much larger number than the loyal men. They were immediately to rise, and every barn and many other buildings were to be set on fire, to overwhelm the people with confusion and terror. The conspirators within the city, well organized, were to unite with the invaders, and thus they expected to obtain easy possession of the public property and of the national Capital.

" A few trusty friends of the Government, visitors in Washington, immediately commenced vigorous but secret measures to assist the Administration in this fearful crisis. They hastened, by committees, to all the hotels, and sought out those known to be true to the Union, informed them of the peril, and appointed a meeting that very evening, in the church in the rear of Willard's Hotel, where they would not attract attention. Solemnly and with intense emotion they administered the oath anew, of fidelity to the national flag, to every one to whom they confided their secret, and then gave to each the pass which would admit him to the church. This work was speedily accomplished, for there was not a moment to be lost, and soon about two hundred men were assembled in the church.

" After listening to a few words of eloquence, which yet burn in the souls of some of the volunteers in that dark night of the nation's peril, the company formed themselves into the noted, ' CASSIUS M. CLAY BATTALION.' These noble men, many of whom were among the most distinguished in wealth and position to be found in our land, were enrolled, under efficient officers, into small patrol parties, and marched all night long, through the streets of the city, to guard against incendiaries, and to prevent the assembling of the conspirators. They had orders to shoot down promptly any who should resist their authority."

Another party of three hundred men were also appointed under Gen. Lane, to repair, unobserved, to the White House, and *bivouac* in the East Room, ready to give a warm reception to any parties who might make a sudden attack upon the Presidential mansion. For three weeks, the East Room was thus occupied. Gen. Scott, with his characteristic promptness, took quiet and unobserved possession of the Capitol, behind whose massive walls a few hundred men could maintain a desperate defense. This magnificent building was immediately stored with provisions and military stores. Thus a citadel was extemporized, into which the General could withdraw the President and his Cabinet, with some chance of maintaining a siege, until troops could fight their way down, for their rescue, from the North. A band of very trusty men were selected to execute these movements, the utmost care being taken to elude the vigilance of the spies and traitors who swarmed on every side.

The whole city was in a state of commotion, for though but few were aware of the definite plans of the conspirators, it was universally known that for months, in Maryland and Virginia, military companies had been organized and drilled, with the avowed object of a raid upon the Capital. Some of these troops were under the guidance of an officer in the regular army, still holding his commission, and receiving his pay. It was openly boasted by the Rebels, that they had five thousand men ready to strike the blow whenever the signal should be given.

The Government, with the very limited means in its possession, was vigilant in guarding against surprise. The long bridge across the Potomac was patrolled by a party of dragoons. A detachment of artillery was also posted, at night, on the Washington side with guns to sweep the bridge.

Lieutenant Jones, of the United States Army, was in command at Harper's Ferry, with but forty-three men. Heroically he made his preparations to blow up the arsenal, should he find the enemy coming upon him in overpowering numbers. At 10 o'clock at night, of the 19th of April, he received positive information, that nearly 3000 State troops, dispatched by Governor Letcher, of Virginia, would reach Harper's Ferry in two hours, approaching from Winchester, and that 300 troops, from Hallstown, were within 20 minutes' march of the arsenal.

The combustibles had been previously prepared, and the torch was at once applied. In three minutes, all the buildings of the armory were in a blaze. The arsenal at the Ferry was in the State of Virginia. Many of the citizens in that vicinity were in league with the conspirators. Lieut. Jones, with his little band of forty men, retreated across the bridge into Maryland, and thence, by a march all night, reached a place of safety in Carlisle, Penn. The Secessionists at the Ferry rushed to the arsenal, in the vain attempt to extinguish the flames. In their rage they then pursued the heroic band, and firing upon them, succeeded in killing two of their number.   Before morning there were nearly 5000 Virginia troops holding the important post.

While the traitorous Letcher was, as Governor of Virginia, executing these plots, the State was still nominally in the Union.   Letcher had not even yet pretended to absolve himself from the oath of allegiance to the Constitution of the United States.

On the 17th of April, a Convention in Virginia, in secret conclave, passed an ordinance of secession.   It was, for a time, kept a profound secret from the community, that measures might be adopted for seizing Fortress Monroe, the Gosport Navy Yard at Norfolk, and the arsenal at Harper's Ferry.   The Virginia rebels immediately sent a *private messenger* to the Confederate Government to inform them of their action.

The Norfolk Navy Yard was one of the most extensive and valuable naval depots in the United States.   Government property was accumulated there to the amount of many millions of dollars.   The spacious yard, three-fourths of a mile long, and one quarter of a mile wide, was covered with machine-shops, founderies, storehouses, and dwellings for the officers.   There were three large ship-houses and a magnificent dry-dock of granite.   In fact it was almost a city in itself of shops and magazines of every kind, and an immense amount of naval and military stores were accumulated there. This all, the land included, was the property of the United States.

But Mr. Floyd, a Virginian, had taken good care that there should be no troops there to defend it; and Mr. Buchanan's Secretary of the Navy had been equally skillful in depriving it of all naval support.   There was then floating in the splendid harbor the new steam frigate Merrimac, which had cost $1,200,000; the Pennsylvania, the largest line-of-battle ship in the world; the Germantown, the Dolphin, and many other noble vessels of war, partially dismantled.   The whole property of the yard was estimated at over 9,000,000 of dollars.   Capt. McCaulay was at that time in command of the yard.   The secession feeling, in Norfolk and Portsmouth, was general and bitter.   Every effort had been made by the conspirators to inflame the populace.   Public meetings were held, in which distinguished speakers urged the claims of what they called Southern Rights, and denounced the General Government.   John Letcher, the Governor of Virginia, in his response to the President's appeal for troops, had said, "The militia of Virginia will not be furnished to the powers at Washington, for any such use or purpose as they have in view.   You have chosen to inaugurate civil war, and, having done so, we will meet it in a spirit as determined, as the Administration has exhibited towards the South."

On the night of the 16th of April, by order of this Governor Letcher, a large number of boats, laden with stones, were sunk in the channel, so as to render it impossible to tow out these large ships.   Immediate arrangements were then made for seizing the yard.   Most of the sub-officers in the yard were traitors from the South, and they baffled all the endeavors of the loyal men to do anything for the protection of the property, and for the honor of the flag of the United States.

As this yard was in the heart of one of the most fanatic of the slave-holding States, many of the workmen were easily won over to the side of rebellion. The military companies of Portsmouth and Norfolk were called out, some batteries were hastily constructed commanding the yard, and on the morning of April 18, the rebel General Taliaferro arrived at Norfolk to take charge of the troops. All things being thus prepared, the rebel naval officers resigned their commissions, and passed over to the service of the Confederates. We doubt whether the history of this world can show, among civilized men, any acts of dishonor, so flagrant. The rebels seemed to have lost all sense of the meaning of the word *honor*.

It was now manifest that the Yard could not be preserved, and that it must fall into the hands of the rebels, with its immense store of war materials, and its three thousand heavy cannon, unless it could be destroyed. Not a moment was to be lost. At 7 o'clock Saturday night, April 21, the steamship Pawnee cast off from the dock at Fortress Monroe, with six hundred trusty men on board, to aid in the destruction of the yard, and to bring off the loyal man. It was a calm, moonlight night. The steamer passed rapidly at the Elizabeth river, winding its way with some difficulty through the sunken vessels which encumbered the channel. About 9 o'clock it reached Gosport Navy Yard. Their arrival was anticipated, and they were received with enthusiastic cheers. The crews of the Cumberland and the Pennsylvania, several hundred in number, were especially hearty in their acclaim. "They welcomed us," said one, "with a hurricane of heartiness."

The traitors were quite surprised at this sudden appearance of the Pawnee, and all the inhabitants of Norfolk and Portsmouth were speedily aroused; the guilty, trembling with the apprehension that their cities were to be bombarded, and the innocent, apprehensive that the insulted Government was about to punish the traitors for their crimes. For a few hours the Pawnee could overawe all resistance. But in a couple of days, rebellious Virginia could send twenty thousand men, well armed, to consummate her treason. It was therefore necessary to act without an hour's delay. The Pawnee made fast to the dock, immediately landed the troops, and seized all the gates of the yard that no foes could enter. The magnificent Pennsylvania could not be towed out over the obstructions of the channel, but it was thought that the Cumberland, of lighter draft, might be saved.

Everything of value in the Pennsylvania and the other vessels, except the heavy guns, was transferred to the Pawnee, and the Cumberland. Busy hands, nearly two thousand in number, worked with intense activity all night long. Everything which could not be removed, and which might prove valuable to the Rebels, the utmost efforts were made to destroy. Shot and shell, revolvers, carbines, stands of arms, were thrown overboard. It is estimated that there were nearly 3000 heavy guns in the yard, many of them columbiads and splendid Dahlgrens. These could only be spiked. They subsequently manned the innumerable batteries of the Rebels, and opened their thunders upon the Stars and Stripes in the disaster at Manassas. This great reservoir became an inexhaustible source of supply to the rebels, and enabled them to bring into the field, at the commencement of the conflict, an armament far superior to any with which the Government could furnish its troops.

The work of destruction and preparations for the great conflagration were prosecuted with unwearied energy, by the light of the moon, until it sank beneath the horizon, about 12 o'clock. The barracks were then set on fire, and the crackling flames, leaping into the sky, illumined the whole scene with almost the glare of day. Four o'clock in the morning came. The combustibles were all arranged, the trains laid, the matches prepared, to set on fire ships, houses, shops—everything that would burn. The Pawnee, taking the Cumberland in tow, and receiving on board the two ships all the men from the yard, excepting a few to fire the trains, left its moorings, ready to depart, and sent up a rocket. The scene which ensued can not be better described than in the language of an eye-witness:

" The rocket sped high in the air, paused a second, and burst in shivers of many colored lights. And as it did so, the well-set trains at the ship-houses, and on the decks of the fated vessels left behind, went off as if lit simultaneously by the rocket. One of the ship-houses contained the old New York, a ship thirty years on the stocks, and yet unfinished. The other was vacant; but both houses and the old New York burned like tinder. The vessels fired were the Pennsylvania, the Merrimac, the Germantown, the Plymouth, the Raritan, the Columbia, the Dolphin. The old Delaware and Columbus, worn-out and dismantled seventy-fours, were scuttled and sunk at the upper docks on Friday.

" I need not try to picture the scene of the grand conflagration that now burst, like the day of judgment, on the startled citizens of Norfolk, Portsmouth, and all the surrounding country. Any one who has seen a ship burn, and knows how, like a fiery serpent, the flame leaps from pitchy deck to smoking shrouds, and writhes to their very top, around the masts that stand like martyrs doomed, can form some idea of the wonderful display that followed. It was not 30 minutes from the time the trains were fired, till the conflagration roared like a hurricane, and the flames from land and water, swayed and met, and mingled together, and darted high, and fell and leaped up again, and by their very motion showed their sympathy with the crackling, crashing roar of destruction beneath.

" But in all this magnificent scene, the old ship Pennsylvania was the center-piece. She was a very giant in death as she had been in life. She was a sea of flame, and when ' the iron had entered her soul,' and her bowels were consuming, then did she spout forth, from every porthole of every deck, torrents, and cataracts of fire, that to the mind of Milton would have represented her a frigate of hell, pouring out unremitting broadsides of infernal fire. Several of her guns were left loaded, but not shotted, and as the fire reached them, they sent out on the startled and morning air minute guns of fearful peal, that added greatly to the alarm that the light of the conflagration had spread through the surrounding country. The Pennsylvania burned like a volcano for five hours and a half, before her mainmast fell. I stood watching the proud but perishing old leviathan, as this emblem of her majesty was about to come down. At precisely 9½ o'clock, the tall tree that stood in her center tottered, and fell, and crushed deep into her burning sides, while a storm of sparks flooded the sky."

The dispatch to the rebels at Richmond announcing the successful sinking of stone vessels in the channel of Elizabeth River says, exultingly, " Thus have we secured for Virginia, three of the best ships in the Navy." They were disappointed; the Pennsylvania was utterly distroyed. The Cumberland escaped. The Merrimac burned to the water's edge, and sunk. She was subsequently raised, and, coated with iron armor, plunged into the Cumberland, and sunk her ; and then, like Judas, appropriately committed suicide. Notwithstanding the immense destruction of property by the fire, still millions were left to strengthen the arm of the rebels.

Geo. B. McClellan

J.C. Fremont.

F. Siegel

Benj. F. Butler;

A. H. Foote

Wᵐ A Buckingham